# Toastmaster's Secret

A Practical Guide to Become a "Competent
Communicator" in Public Speaking

## Ramakrishna Reddy

**PublicSpeakKing**

# Disclaimer

Toastmasters International, the Toastmasters International logo, and all other Toastmasters International trademarks and copyrights are the sole property of Toastmasters International. This book is the opinion of the author and is independent of Toastmasters International. It is not authorized by, endorsed by, sponsored by, affiliated with, or otherwise approved by Toastmasters International.

No part of this publication or the information in it may be quoted from or reproduced in any form by means such as printing, scanning, photocopying, or otherwise without prior written permission of the copyright holder. Efforts have been made to ensure that the information in this book is accurate and complete. However, the author and the publisher do not warrant the accuracy of the information, text and graphics contained within the book. The author and the publisher do not hold any responsibility for errors, omissions, or contrary interpretations of the subject matter herein. This book is presented solely for motivational and informational purposes.

# Testimonial from World Champion Of Public Speaking

"is a great mentor to a new Toastmaster. It complements the Toastmaster Competent Communicator Manual and gives the user ideas and insights into how to address stops and barriers they may experience and move efficiently through their initial Toastmasters Communication training."

–Lance Miller
2005 World Champion of Public Speaking
www.lancemillerspeaks.com

Dedicated to the wonderful world of Toastmasters

# About the Author

Ramakrishna Reddy has written multiple books related to public speaking and career. More than 100,000 readers have downloaded his books across formats. He has won 25 speech contests (in India, and the United States) conducted by an international organization for leadership and communication.

Apart from working on projects, playing with his son, and spending quality time (which may include high-volume discussions) with his wife, he coaches professionals to take their public speaking skills to the next level using simple-to-understand, easy-to-implement methods. He can be reached at Rama@PublicSpeakKing.com.

# Also by Ramakrishna Reddy

### <u>Non-Fiction</u>

*The Ultimate Public Speaking Survival Guide*
*Public Speaking Essentials*
*Public Speaking Topic Secrets*
*Connect Using Humor and Story*
*Confessions of a Software Techie*
*Write Effective Emails at Work*

### <u>Fiction</u>

*Perfect Promotion*

# Contents

# Introduction

I wrote this book with just one goal. I want to share fluff-free, practical, and actionable insights. This book is the essence of the learnings from several hundred hours of effort invested in my speech projects on the competent communication track and the learnings I had from speech contests.

If you are a brand new Toastmaster, this is definitely for you. I wish I had access to something like this when I started. Even if you are a fairly seasoned Toastmaster, this book will help strengthen the fundamental speaking elements. If you are interested in knowing the fundamentals of speech creation, preparation, and delivery, this book will be of great help.

As a token of appreciation for picking this book, please enjoy the gifts, which include ready-to-go templates for informative and persuasive speeches, a mini-book on humor, and a surprise (hint: one of my books that'll perfectly complement Toastmaster's Secret!). Visit http://publicspeakking.com/toastmasterssecret/ and follow the instructions on the webpage.

If you are a Toastmaster, skip this part and jump into the chapters. If you are not part of Toastmasters, I strongly recommend you join a good Toastmasters club. Toastmasters is one of the real-time, learn-by-doing programs (there's a membership fee but worth it) that is present all around the world to hone leadership and communication skills. Please visit http://reports.Toastmasters.org/findaclub/ to find a club near you.

Do you take things slow or fast? Taking it slow helps in systematic growth. But from experience, I realized you might fall prey to procrastination. This book is going to help you break the blocks. Any good book will provide you with all the good information and insights. The secret is to use them! Let's begin the journey towards becoming a competent communicator in public speaking. I am excited for you!

**Ramakrishna Reddy**

# Chapter One

# Ice Breaker

Talking about *you* is one of the easiest things to do. But, talking about *you* from a stage might not seem easy. When you want to put your speech on paper, are you raising the following concerns?

1. I don't know what to say.
2. My life is not at all interesting.
3. What would others think of me?
4. Will the audience be impressed?
5. What if I forget my speech?
6. I have so much to say. How can I do it in 4-6 minutes?

If you raised any of the above concerns or a variation of the above, you are not alone. I had more questions. I took an insane amount of time to write my Ice Breaker speech. Guess how much time I took? Four months. Then my mentor called me for a lunch meeting. He did motivate me to take my speech and do something about it but I felt bad. Why? He did not pay for the lunch!

Let us see the objectives of an Ice Breaker speech:

a. To begin speaking before an audience.

b. To discover speaking skills you already have and skills that need some attention.

The objectives seem to be simple and clear. This project is the perfect opportunity to explore more about you.

*Here's the simple idea.* Just answer the questions that I'll share in a few seconds. But before you start, please promise me that you will answer them with stories and not just one-liners. Keep in mind; that you are not obligated to share any information that you don't want to share.

a. How did you come into this world? Where were you born? Place? Situation? Any interesting detail?

b. How was your childhood? Some questions that will help explore your childhood could be: Where did you grow up? Which school did you go to? How were your mom and dad? Were they strict? Were they kind? Were you pampered?

c. Did you have siblings? How were they? Fighting, caring, inspiring, etc.?

d. Was there any person who influenced you in your life? How and when?

e. What would your friends say if a third person asks them about you? Get that information. (Note: You might be amazed by the feedback.)

f.  What are your aspirations? Future goals?

g. What do you believe in? What is your message to the world? Yes, you can become a world leader now. It's your stage!

## SPEECH SCRIPT & ANALYSIS (in bold):

*Title:* My Story

**Starting with an amusing story with a little bit of curiosity helps to engage the audience. Based on this opening, they know that I am stubborn and naughty.**

In a busy market, a boy asked his sisters for an ice cream. When the boy did not get the ice cream, he threw tantrums and rolled on the ground inside the ice cream shop.

This boy was not willing to get up from the floor.

**Introducing my three sisters as characters in the story. It also answered the curiosity: *Why did he tell that story?***

Finally, he had to be dragged home all along the road by his sisters.

This boy was not doing this because his sisters had refused to buy him the ice cream or the shopkeeper didn't have any ice cream. The reason was that the boy did not get his favorite grape-flavored ice cream.

The characters in the story were my three lovely sisters and me.

**Introducing parents here. You can expand here if needed.**

Speaking of family; my dad is an electrical contractor and our breadwinner and my mom is a perfect homemaker.

**Here I am answering the questions about my school education and how I spent my time. You can think about how you spent your time during your childhood.**

I studied at St. Mary's School in Chennai. At least twice a week, I attended the morning school assembly outside the entry gate. I used to be late! In those times, Chennai's scorching sun, just 45 C, also could not stop us from playing on the streets. I used to get into any kind of game.

**Telling the audience something unexpected. They would not have expected me to fly kites!**

Flying kites was also another great sport of mine.

**If you talk to any middle-class Indian guy, your Icebreaker is incomplete without stories about class ranks and comparisons!**

I was not the #1 rank holder in my class, but I maintained my rank within 10 in a class of 50. I was this jolly go-to kid until an incident happened.

**I had a specific story to tell. I chose this story because it had an impact on my life. You also can tell a story that had a profound impact on your life.**

In 9th grade, during a chat with my classmates regarding student rankings in the class, this guy Vivek told me, "Rama, how can you beat my rank?" And I casually replied,

"Come on, if I study hard, I can beat your rank." Vivek replied, "You can never beat my rank." I felt like someone slapped me right on my right cheek. Those words kept inspiring me whenever I picked up a book. On a normal day, I would doze off whenever I opened a book. Then I proved him wrong. Not only did I beat him but I also secured the 2nd rank in the class. That was when I realized I could raise my potential to achieve my target.

**There is a transition to rankings and into college education. I am using a chronological model here. You can follow this and use your incidents.**

I didn't stop there. I consistently maintained my ranks till my 12th standard and got competitive cut-offs for engineering admissions. I got into a chemical engineering department only because I could get into Anna University, Chennai, which is one of the best engineering campuses in India. I had to compete with the best students and achieve good grades.

**Transitioning into my career. I am answering questions such as "How did I feel when I got the job?" and "How do I feel now?" Hope this is helping you get some creative ideas for your icebreaker.**

During my final year placements, I got an offer from one of the best software firms. There was a tingling in my stomach when I joined the company. I used to question if I would survive in the IT software field. I not only survived but also thrived in this industry.

**I am mentioning some traits of mine that I wanted to share.**

There are two significant traits that I would like to share about me. I wake up at 5 in the morning. I jog, practice meditation, and then take a steam bath. I would love to tell you that is my routine activity.

But unfortunately, I have to tell you that I don't do things until the 11th hour. It all started at school, going late and getting spanked by my principal, going late to college, and not entering the class. Even now I wake up at 7:30 a.m. and catch a bus at 7:50 a.m. Well, I would definitely not get into the details of how I manage to get ready.

**I still believe in this and I think this is the most satisfying feeling one can get. What is it that you believe in? Be honest and your audience will love you.**

I believe that helping people with their difficulties is the most satisfying feeling.

I also wish I could be a correct judge of myself while doing so. This is one trait that helps me win real friends.

**Telling a story that was close to my heart to support that point about my trait.**

During the final semester, around 10 people mostly who had current arrears, a history of arrears, or who were from a non-English background were not placed. I was the placement representative of my department and felt badly responsible for them not getting a job offer. After a lot of failed attempts, finally, through our alumni, I came to know about a job opening in a design company. Five students who didn't have current arrears were shortlisted and called for an interview. Contrary to my expectations, the company selected all five students. You feel good about yourself when someone smiles because of you and you keep smiling all day.

**This is a thank-you conclusion to all the people in my life. You can come up with something similar or something else. Maybe you can tell your ambition or future goals.**

I take this as an opportunity to thank each and every person who came into my life till now, who knowingly or unknowingly influenced me in shaping my attitude.

## TECHNIQUES FOR DELIVERY:

So, do you have your script ready? Good job. Let's get going into the delivery part. The following steps are mentioned because I am assuming you are brand-new to public speaking. If you are already comfortable on the stage, you can ignore steps that do not make sense to you.

1. Go to a mirror with your script. Read out as loud as you can. The reason I am telling you to do this is because I want you to get comfortable hearing and projecting your voice. If you have zero or less stage experience, the above exercise might be really helpful. If you want to use a wall-size mirror, fitness center mirrors in your community would help (make sure you practice when no one else is using the fitness center!) for this activity. In the corporate world, washroom mirrors also can do the job but you might need to practice during off hours or else you might freak out people coming to the restroom/washroom!

2. Even though you can use notes, I recommend against using them. Here's a simple technique. Connect the images of the speech in your mind and speak out (we will use a better technique in the next project). In the speech example, if you look closely, you can dice the speech into frames.

*First picture*: A street with a shop on one side and my house on the other side. My 3 sisters and I are buying from the store and then they drag me. Can you map this in a single frame?

*Second picture*: I am standing outside the entry gate at school. Getting spanked and going late to school regularly.

*Third picture:* Playing in the streets, flying kites, and hanging around with no aim in life!

3. Once you are comfortable with the script, deliver this speech to your family, close friends, or anyone who will listen to your speech!

*Steps to take on the day of your speech:*

4. Get excited to deliver your story. If you can do this one thing, you will be awesome on stage!

5. Ask your club member or fellow Toastmaster to record your Ice Breaker speech.

6. A minute before you are called on stage, your heart might race, your hands might shiver, your legs might wobble, you might feel the urge to go to the restroom, and all weird things will happen. If these things do not happen, either you have some experience in public speaking or you are a born speaker! When they do happen, rub your left palm with your right hand for 10-15 seconds and vice versa. Bring your heart rate to normal. Slowly, breathe in and breathe out. Now go ahead and enjoy the delivery.

*Steps to take after you deliver your speech:*

7. After your speech, listen to your evaluations. Get feedback on your speech. Again, all evaluations are not perfect. As my favorite mentor, Jerry Aiyathurai (World Championship of Public Speaking finalist) says, "Take it if you like it; else cheerfully ignore it." Keep in mind; that you might get certain feedback for which you are not even ready. For example, if your current pressing problem is wobbling legs, you might get feedback on voice modulation as well. In such a case, you

have to work on overcoming wobbling legs before working on voice modulation.

8. Collect your video recording. You might be happy or not so happy with your speech delivery. Do not get discouraged or form opinions by watching your video. Every speaker started from somewhere. Your recording is the precious information to help you grow. In the delivery techniques part of the next chapter, I will tell you what to do with your recording.

# Chapter Two

# Organize Your Speech

Any content you read, whether it is prose, poetry, article, newsletter, or story; always has one thing in common. When you are casually sharing something with your friends, talking about an experience, you will observe that there is again one thing in common. And that is called **structure**. It's the structure that'll *hold your speech together*.

Let us see the objectives of this project:

a. Select an appropriate outline, which allows listeners to easily follow and understand your speech.

b. Make your message clear, with supporting material directly contributing to that message.

c. Use appropriate transitions when moving from one idea to another.

d. Create a strong opening and conclusion.

My speech topic for Organize Your Speech was *Sleep*. I selected this topic after days and days of deliberation. I generally used to spend a lot of days looking for a perfect topic for my speech. I would eventually come up with one and then I would spend days and days to finally come up with a reason why my audience would not be impressed with that topic. I later realized that project speeches are meant for experience, and not to impress someone. Learn from me: don't waste time selecting a topic. Your main aim is to speak on stage. To quote Darren LaCroix, 2001 World Champion of Public Speaking: "Stage time, stage time, and stage time."

I have given an excerpt from my book Public Speaking Topic Secrets in chapter 11. Please go through the same and find a topic quickly. If you are still not able to, please check out the book Public Speaking Topic Secrets. A lot of my students have been successful in finding a speech topic after reading that book.

## SPEECH SCRIPT & ANALYSIS (in bold):

The speech follows the below structure.

Opening

Transition

What are we talking about?

Part 1

 Section 1

 Section 2

 Section 3

Part 2

The benefit of the subject

Drawbacks of not following the theme

Conclusion

   *Title*: Something to ponder

**Starting with a story is my favorite technique for opening a speech. You can use any other technique such as a question or a statistic, as long as they capture the audience's attention. One of my mentees whistled a tune as the opening for his speech and the audience loved it. Please use your imagination to grab your audience's attention.**

It was my database management training class. Mr. Venky, our highly enthusiastic tutor, advanced to the first row of the class and repeated the same concept again and again in a louder tone. This unusual act caught everyone's attention in the class. Vamsi, my friend who sat next to me, was nudging me so that I would open my eyes. To my horror, I realized that our tutor was standing right in front of me and shouting the concept. He was trying to wake me up.

**Please observe the transition. I told a story in my introduction about an incident in which I was sleeping. Then I am introducing the topic of *Sleep*.**

Mr. Toastmaster, fellow Toastmasters, and dear guests, the reason why I told my classroom incident was not to justify why I am dumb in database management concepts but to illustrate the point that I did not have enough sleep the previous night. All living things are subject to this phenomenon called "Sleep."

**I am transitioning into the details of *Sleep* with a question.**

Have you ever wondered what causes sleep?

**Transitioning into the core subject. Giving them an idea about the subject.**

Let me explain. Sleep occurs based on the biological clock. We have dedicated sensors on the retina that deliver the day-time/nighttime message directly to a gland tucked deep inside the brain. In response to darkness, this tiny brain tissue produces the sleep-inducing hormone melatonin, broadcasting the message to brain areas that govern everything from body temperature to protein synthesis to hormone production to alertness.

**I am engaging the audience so that they don't sleep! Dividing the subject into two parts. The first part is divided into three sections. Now we have to talk about those parts and sections.**

Have you ever wondered what exactly happens when we hit the sack?

**Explaining the first point.**

Once we close our eyes, we are subjected to two types of sleep.

The first one is NREM sleep (Non Rapid Eye Movement). This is the dreamless sleep. The NREM sleep has three major stages:

Drowsiness is Stage 1. It lasts just for 5 or 10 minutes. And in this stage our eyes move slowly under the eyelids, muscle activity slows down and we are easily awakened.

**Explaining the second point.**

Stage 2 is Light Sleep. In this stage, our eye movements stop, heart rate reduces, and body temperature decreases.

**Explaining the third point.**

At Stage 3, we reach Deep Sleep. It becomes difficult to awaken us at this stage. If somebody tries to do that and succeeds, we do not adjust immediately and often feel groggy and disoriented for several minutes. I was told that I refused to move out of my room when my friend Albin tried to wake me up when there were earthquake tremors. Deep sleep allows the brain to go on a little vacation needed to restore the energy we expend during our waking hours.

**Explaining the second section of the speech.**

The next type of sleep is the REM (Rapid Eye Movement) sleep where our brain is active as it was when we were awake. Our body temperature rises; the forebrain starts working – trying to analyze random information thrown before it. In other words, we are in dreamland. My parents used to tell me that while sleeping I used to shout something like "Howzaaaat... Catch it quick... hit it." I always thought that something was wrong with me, but recently only I realized it was all due to the mechanism of REM sleep. REM is the period when we fly without wings, we spend without earning, and our most fancied wishes and desires come true.

**Talking about the benefits of the topic.**

Each sleep stage is important for the overall quality of sleep, but deep sleep and REM sleep are especially vital. During deep sleep blood flow decreases to the brain and redirects towards the muscles, restoring physical energy. It is this time when our immune system gets some time to be healed. Have you ever observed that whenever you are done with a big project or series of exams, you get cold or experience body pain? Well, at least now you should know this is not an accident and is mostly due to a lack of deep sleep. REM sleep helps in cell division and protein synthesis, which aid in repairing the muscles; human growth hormone is also released during sleep. This is the reason why children should sleep more hours.

**Sharing possible reasons for the adverse situation and reflecting the seriousness of the issue.**

The biggest sleep robber of all, however, is work. The puritan ethic has gone haywire in an era of global markets. To accommodate the relentless pressure for productivity, we're sleeping less and spending less time in social and leisure pursuits, which results in more stress and can steal away even more sleep.

**Conclusion: Conveying the idea that I am going to perform these actions and indirectly telling the audience to do these in order to enjoy getting the benefits of sleep.**

I am not sure if it's feasible for you all to heed my request to go to sleep on time and maintain consistent sleeping habits. But I will go home, have a hot bath, eat simple food, and have a good night's sleep so that I feel energetic and fully alert to take on tomorrow's challenge.

## TECHNIQUES FOR DELIVERY:

Do you have a recording of your earlier speech? Do you see any of the below?

· Hand shivers
· Wobbling of legs
· Repetitive gesturing of hands
· Walking left and right like a pendulum

· Shifting weight of body on right or left leg at regular intervals

· Slouchy shoulders

· Looking down during the speech

· Not making eye contact with the audience or looking at the ceiling

· Monotone voice

· Showing tension in the face while narrating a pleasant experience

· Laughing even before the audience laughs after telling a joke

· Not showing emotions that correspond to the intent of the message

Maybe you don't exhibit any of the above or you exhibit some of them. I am going to tell you something important. You might hear the advice, "Practice again and again." We need to know what, how, and how long to practice. First and foremost, identify the *areas of distraction* in your delivery. Then, practice *to avoid* those distractions. I am not telling you to work on body language or voice modulation (there are different projects later). For this project, all I want you to do is practice *to avoid* any distracting mechanisms that you identified from your speech recording.

How do you do that?

When you rehearse your speech for this project, ask your friend or fellow Toastmaster to look for any distractions. If your friends are busy, as an alternative, please self-record your speech while rehearsing. (Use a laptop with an inbuilt microphone and camera for this. It works like a charm.) Look for any distractions. Note them down and make a conscious effort to remove those distractions while rehearsing your speech.

The idea of delivering a polished and classy speech boils down to delivering that rehearsed speech *naturally*. Have you watched Steve Jobs speak in a conversational tone during his product launches? Steve Jobs used to practice for hours before the product launch speeches. Don't you think Steve Jobs knew enough about his products? Don't you think there is some logic in practicing your speech beforehand? If you don't practice at this stage, you may need to practice harder later.

I will give two practical techniques to step up your delivery.

1. If you know the room where you are going to speak, then go to that room the previous day. Take a good look at the empty chairs or seats. If you have time and if the situation permits, please practice your speech in that room. After returning home or when you are back to your usual practice location, do the below:

a. Close your eyes and imagine the presentation room to be occupied by people.

b. With your eyes still closed, start practicing your speech by talking with them. Practicing with closed eyes is something I learned from Craig Valentine (1999 World Champion of Public Speaking) through one of his audio programs. This technique has personally helped me a lot. I have used this when I am practicing for my contests.

2. I want to introduce you to another favorite practice technique of mine. If you do this, you will be far, far ahead of

other speakers. Ready for this? You practice till *your speech is in your muscle memory*. What do I mean by this? You can feel that your speech is in your muscle memory if you don't have to focus on your next thought or word during speech delivery. When you keep drilling your speech again and again, after some time, the speech gets into your blood, and you no longer need to recall your speech. When you are in this sweet spot, your conviction and sincerity will show for itself. You'll get excited and start saying, "I can't wait to deliver this speech"!

Please don't forget to:

1. Practice, Practice, Practice.

2. Record your speech when you deliver your speech before the audience.

# Chapter Three

# Get to the Point

D id you ever get bored of something? Have you heard people say, "That's boring"?

Why does this happen?

Well, the majority of the time it is because they did not *get the point*. It could be about a movie, a conversation, or an article.

Do you realize the importance of getting to the point? Would it be a good idea to master this skill?

I think *Getting to the Point* was key for me to understand the core fundamentals of speech creation and speech writing.

**Getting to the point in a speech should be directly proportional to the clarity of your message.**

Let us get to the objectives:

a. Select a speech topic and determine its general and specific purpose.

b. Organize the speech.

c. Ensure that the beginning, body and conclusion reinforce those purposes.

d. Project sincerity and conviction.

e. Strive not to use notes.

Let us see how you can come up with a general and specific purpose. The Toastmasters Competent Communicator manual suggests the general purpose can be of four types:

1. Informational

2. Persuasive (or motivational)

3. Humorous (or entertaining)

4. Inspirational

How to select general purpose?

It depends on your requirements. If you just want to inform the audience, then write down the key points and construct the speech accordingly. If you want to entertain the audience, then add humor to your speech. But practically, the general purpose is not something that is 100% Informative, 100% entertaining,  or 100% persuasive, or 100% inspirational. It is usually a combination of 2 or more different types in the above list. (For entertaining speeches, you need to know concepts of humor and joke creation. Please visit http://publicspeakking.com/toastmasterssecret/ to download a mini-book "Humor Creation Made Simple" along with other useful guides).

What is the Specific Purpose?

The specific purpose is the thesis or the one-line message of your speech. Craig Valentine, 1999 World Champion of Public Speaking, says you should be able to summarize your speech on the back of a business card. What he means is that your speech should have a clear purpose for what the audience should feel, do, or think after listening to your speech.

As discussed in the earlier chapter, please check out the excerpt from my book Public Speaking Topic Secrets in chapter 11. Please go through the same and find a topic quickly. If you are still not able to, please check out the book Public Speaking Topic Secrets.

## SPEECH SCRIPT & ANALYSIS (in bold):

The outline used here is:

Opening

Transition into topic

Engage the audience

Story 1

Insight or/and Opinion

Story 2 (you could continue story 1)

Insight or/and Opinion

Story 3

Insight or/and Opinion

Summarization

Conclusion

Title: Embarrassments

**My opening is a story with subtle humor. Observe that this story leads or transitions to my specific purpose, "Laugh at yourself during embarrassment."**

Last week, en route to office, my bike stuttered for a while and then conked out. After examining it, I found out that the vehicle had run out of fuel. Unfortunately, that day my sweet but dashing friend Neha was traveling with me. While I was figuring out my options to solve the issue, Neha fired a question: "Rama, what is your plan of action?" My manager usually asks a question of this nature. It was quite an embarrassing situation considering the fact that I didn't have any action plan.

**Introducing the theme of my speech.**

I smiled at her and laughed at myself.

**I am involving the audience so that they are hooked to my speech.**

Mr. Toastmaster, fellow Toastmasters, and dear guests, most of us at one point or the other in our lives would have faced an embarrassing situation. And probably we ended up blushing and cursing ourselves or even others.

**This transition poses a question to the audience to make them think.**

But the million-dollar question is how many times did we laugh at ourselves?

**Start of story 1. Use a story that has relevance to your main point. It can be a sub-point to the main point. But choose one that makes sense. A little secret: Use personal stories. They can help you to easily connect with your audience.**

I distinctly remember my first public appearance, when I was in my 2nd grade. My English teacher Alma in her sweet and shrill voice announced, "Students, we have our elocution competition next week." The class went abuzz. At that point, I did not have the slightest idea of what the competition was about or what you do in it. Just to show off, amidst the admiring glances of my classmates, I went forward and submitted my name for the competition. Later, my sister explained me about the elocution competition. The topic was "Time and tide wait for none." Then I memorized the speech, which she wrote for me. The D-day arrived. The auditorium was packed to full house. I was called on stage. I held the mike and started my speech, "Time is a gift given by God. One has to use it as a tool and not a crutch and... Dei. Naaye. Sollrra. Naaye," these whispers in English can be translated to "Hey idiot, dog! Come on, tell, just tell." Instead of my speech, my whisper was amplified to the audience. What next? I had no option but to tell them "thank you" and disappear in sheer embarrassment. That was my first public appearance, rather a public embarrassment.

**These are the insights (key points) from that personal experience.**

Instead of accepting the fact that I was not prepared, I was trying to deliver my speech by swearing at myself. Subsequently, those swearing words were amplified to the audience. This proved to be more embarrassing than the fact that I forgot my speech. There I got my first lesson: Attempting to force out of the situation would add more embarrassment.

**I am telling my current opinion of that situation. You see, just telling a story won't help the audience. Your *point of view* is what they want to know. I had used this unknowingly but after researching and watching great speakers, I can vouch for this point.**

Today, when I recollect that experience, I cannot stop laughing at myself.

**Story 2. The best way to transition here is to move to a different part of the stage. More on this in Project 5 but it makes sense to practice this if you get an opportunity.**

During my first year of college, another interesting thing happened. My English professor was explaining technical writing and giving practical tips to improve the same. I was sitting behind the topper of my class Nishaanti. Instead of listening to the class I was trying to catch a glimpse of the pictures on the magazine she was furtively reading. Suddenly, my professor called me out: "Rama, what are you doing?"

Well, I was perplexed and stood up.

She asked, "Are you a scholar in technical writing?"

I said, "No."

"Then why are you not taking notes?"

I looked around. To my surprise, the whole class except me and Nishaanti were taking notes. Gosh! She went on, "Why do you come to my class? Why don't you just stay out if you know everything?" While I was getting scolded, Nishaanti quickly opened her notebook and acted as if she was taking notes. Once the professor went out of the class, my friends again took me for a ride.

**An insight into my second story. A pun and a humorous touch will help to keep your audience engaged.**

I was unhappy and furious at that point because my self-image had taken a beating. What would my classmates, especially the girls, think of me? These questions made me unhappy.

**My current opinion on this theme.**

Today I have learned that accepting the embarrassing situation "as it is" is usually the best thing, rather than worrying about our self-image. I can't stop laughing when I think about that incident.

**Story 3. This is an excerpt from one of the greatest epics in the world. I love this example and the observation. I could very easily convey my third lesson relating to my specific purpose. Even if you do not know the epic *Mahabharata*, I think I have constructed the story so that anyone can understand the substance.**

In the great epic *Mahabharata*, Kaurava prince Duryodhan fell into a water pond disguised as Rangoli art. In spite of the warning, he fell into the pond. Pandava queen Dhrowpathi laughed at Duryodhan referring to him as blind because of his stupidity. Duryodhan developed a doom and gloom or a rather negative mindset to take revenge on Pandavas and Dhrowpathi. Duryodhan's approach resulted in his defeat or rather the defeat of his kingdom. Instead, if Duryodhan had accepted his stupidity and if he had laughed at himself, who knows, maybe, the Kurukshetra war wouldn't have been fought. This incident from *Mahabharata* tells us, "When caught in an embarrassing situation, developing a negative mindset would prove to be futile."

**I am summarizing the 3 lessons into a single specific purpose and making my message clear for the audience. More depth is added by playing with the quotation "To err is human."**

These 3 lessons point to one thing: Laugh at yourself. The simple reason why we don't laugh at ourselves is we all want to be perfect. And in that quest for achieving perfection, we don't want others to see our embarrassments. We all know that *to err is human.* By changing just two letters, we can learn that *to err is humor.* Who knows when we might face another embarrassment?

**In conclusion, I end the speech on a positive note by telling the audience about the benefits of *following the specific purpose of the speech.***

So accept the embarrassment lightheartedly and be excited and happy because you are getting a chance to laugh at yourself once again.

## TECHNIQUES FOR DELIVERY:

Since this project focuses on speech writing and creation, I think you are good if you follow the delivery techniques outlined in the earlier chapters. Please don't forget to:

1. Practice, Practice, Practice.

2. Record your speech when you deliver your project before the audience.

# Chapter Four

# How to Say It

In life, we decide, learn, and judge by communicating with others. We form perceptions, we get inspired, and we even get influenced based on words. Can you imagine the power of words? Wouldn't it be great to learn how to use them effectively? To be honest, it was this project that honed my speech-writing skills to the next level. I never imagined that words could add so much beauty to the ideas I wanted to communicate.

Let us see the objectives of this project:

a. Select the right words and sentence structure to communicate your ideas clearly, accurately, and vividly.

b. Use rhetorical devices to enhance and emphasize ideas.

c. Eliminate jargon and unnecessary words. Use correct grammar.

Since the project required the use of words to convey your ideas accurately and vividly, I started thinking about some stories where there was excitement and thrill. Then, I remembered my travel to my friend's wedding from one city to another. This project forced me to look into www .thesaurus.com and www.dictionary.com to find the *exact* meaning of every word. It is fascinating how the usage of the right word at the right time can leave a lasting impression in the minds of your audience. This is the project where you will hone your writing skills. I learned the effective use of rhetorical devices such as simile, metaphor, and alliteration. I also learned how to use words that are pleasing to sensory perceptions. Though not required, it was the first project where I tried my hand at humor. People did not laugh out loud but they were giggling and smiling.

For this project, more effort should be spent on polishing the speech script with the right words. Use www.thesaurus.com and www.dictionary.com to find the right words. Repeating it: Delaying your project in the name of topic selection is the last thing you want to do. Please check out chapter 11 or if you want more, please refer to the book Public Speaking Topic Secrets for finding relevant topics.

## SPEECH SCRIPT & ANALYSIS (in bold)

*Title:* An Unforgettable Ride

**The whole speech was a single story. Hence, Opening by default is a story.**

Last November, my friend Alin and I decided to board a blue horse, which departed Pune sharply at 12:10 in the morning.

**Observe the use of metaphor: Horse is used as a metaphor for the train 'Dadar Express'. Painting a picture by saying**

**it was blue in color (Color helps the audience visualize better).**

This horse was Dadar Express, the train from Mumbai to Chennai via Pune. I agreed to pick up my friend Alin at Khadkee and hit the road to the railway station. Before the travel, I went to attend my co-worker's marriage party. The marriage was so vibrant and colorful that I lost track of time.

Mr. Toastmaster, fellow Toastmasters, and dear guests, time didn't pause.

**As you can see, there are no loose ends to the sentences. The sentences were specific: 10:55 p.m., 400 bucks, 11:55 p.m., what was I going through, what was my friend going through.**

Only at 10:55 p.m. I remembered about my travel. I bustled through the crowd and ran out of the hall to catch a taxi. My heartbeat was rising as I was racing against time. At 11:20 p.m., I hired a taxi for 400 bucks. By pestering the driver to throttle to maximum speed, I reached Khadkee at 11:55 p.m. Alin was frantically waiting for me in the middle of the road.

**To make it more lively and interesting, please note the use of dialogue, specific words such as 'bawled', and the use of contrast between 'cold' and 'warmth'.**

At first glance, Alin bawled, "I think we are too early for the next day's train."

The stage was set. The driver got a perfect ground to showcase his driving skills. The taxi blazed in full throttle again and I started shivering on that cold winter night. My only source of warmth was Alin's hot scolding.

**Please note the use of direct verbs in most cases: came, carried, paid, and galloped**

At 12:08, the taxi came to a screeching halt near the Meridian End of Pune station. I carried the bag, Alin paid the money, and we galloped.

**I'm a big fan of Triad, and below is a good example of its use.**

We jostled through the crowd, dashed through the Railway Protection Force, and reached platform 6.

**Alliteration (it's the use of similar-sounding syllables to create a great listening experience) is a powerful rhetorical device: railway rules, cut across**

Alin shouted, "Look, Mumbai- Chennai Dadar Express on platform 4." Violating railway rules, we cut across the railway track and boarded the 3-tier AC coach. On my way to the compartment, a gentleman approached me and asked "Son, when will this train reach Mumbai?" I confidently replied, "Sir!!! This train is heading towards Chennai. You have boarded the wrong train." A middle-aged lady near me sarcastically said, "Hey, excuse me. This train is heading towards Mumbai." Hearing that, I almost reeled. My watch struck 12:10; I grabbed the bag and rushed out screaming, "Alin, run!!!! Find out our train!"

Before I could explain, we saw the blue twin brother on platform no. 2.

**The sentences come to life when words are visual (the audience can see) and vocal (the audience can hear). And also, I mixed this with the use of alliteration. (See italics.)**

**It resulted in a beautiful sentence "We saw the signal turn green..."**

We *saw the signal* turn green and *heard the heavy* siren blow. Subsequently, the train started.

**Please note the use of simile: referencing a famous Hindi movie scene to show the action in the speech.**

Finally, like Kareena Kapoor boarding the Mumbai-Delhi Express in *Jab We Met*, we boarded the Mumbai-Chennai Dadar Express.

**Here, I use sensory words that touch visual senses: red T-shirt, well-built guys.**

We got into our compartment, to see a group of well-built guys showing off their muscles to their girlfriends. We stared at them conspicuously. One guy wearing a red T-shirt came close by. "What is the issue, Boss?" I responded, "We have two berths reserved in this compartment." Immediately the clan clamored, "Here!!! No, no. You boarded the wrong compartment. Check your ticket." Alin shot back, "What? We have booked in this compartment only. Let me clarify." Saying this, Alin went in search of the Railway Inspector. I had nothing much to do except watch the pretty girls in the compartment.

After 15 minutes, Alin called, "Tickets have been escalated to 2 tier B1 coach. Hey, one more issue, the intermediate coach has been shut to passengers." I said, "Then, please cross over when the train halts at any station. I will go to B1 coach and settle down." Alin got stuck in a different compartment like Shahrukh Khan got stuck in the movie *Dilwale Dulhania Le Jayenge*. At B1, the coach assistant warned me not to open the coach doors as we entered the area of notorious dacoits.

**Please note the use of adjectives: cozy blanket, hush silence.**

After he left, I let myself into the cozy blanket. In a while, my cell phone rang and broke the hushed silence in the compartment. Alin said, "The train stopped for signal clearance. I would come over to B1 coach." I said, "Do not get off the train. Hey, hey. Do not," and the call got disconnected. I put my phone on silent to avoid further disturbance in the compartment.

**Below is the use of words for visual and auditory senses: saw dark woods, heard pin-drop silence.**

I glanced through the window. I saw dark woods and heard pin-drop silence.

While the warning regarding the dacoits was lingering in my mind, I noticed my cell phone flashing. I saw 4 missed calls in a span of just 1 minute from Alin.

**Action words fill the speech with drama and excitement: bellow, rushed, peeped, commotion.**

As soon as I attended the fifth call, my left eardrum suffered from a bellow, "Hey, idiot. Why didn't you pick up the call? What the hell are you doing?" I rushed to the right door of the B1 coach. I peeped out along the length of the train. It was pitch-dark. Meanwhile, on call, I heard, "Hey!!! Someone ... shooting. Hey. Hey. Don't..." Nervously, I opened the left door of the coach. I witnessed a group racing on the track with a lot of commotion.

In the background, flashlights were flying in all directions. I said, "Alin, I can see some *drama* here. I could see the Railway Protection Force chasing some dacoits. I should shut the door. You are safe, right?'

Alin yelled, "Dumb idiot. That's me. I am the one who is running towards the door. Open the door. Open the door."

In the end, we both explained the issue to Railway Police and settled in our compartment. We didn't exchange a word for a few minutes but ultimately burst out into a hefty laughter.

Even though the incident turned out to be an adventure, I came up with three valuable lessons.

1. Leave the party on time before travel.

2. Make sure your travel arrangements are good.

3. Do not make decisions hastily.


## TECHNIQUES FOR DELIVERY:

Since this project's focus is on improving your writing skills, I think you are good if you follow the delivery techniques given in the earlier chapters.

Please don't forget to:

1. Practice, Practice, Practice.

2. Record your speech when you deliver your project before the audience.

# Chapter Five

# Body Language

According to research, words only account for 7% of communication. The remaining 93% caters to body language and vocal variety. There is some controversy around the exact percentage of verbal and non-verbal. We need not argue about that. Why? Based on experience and common sense, we can safely agree that words alone do not influence the communication process. This means that non-verbal communication plays a much more important role in your communication with your audience. And your body language has a lion's share in your non-verbal communication.

Let us see the speech objectives:

a. Use stance, movement, facial expressions, and eye contact to express your message and achieve your speech's purpose.

b. Make your body language smooth and natural.

After my project on *How to Say It*, there was a storytelling competition in my club. I decided to write a story about an exciting trip with my friends. I won the contest. I thought about it. Why not use the same speech to deliver my project on *Body Language*? It worked out very well because the story had a lot of scope to showcase different elements of body language. People remember the speech even after several years. So it'll help if you choose an adventurous story for this project.

Based on the objectives, you can choose speech topics that have scope for physical movement, action, drama, and dialogue. Yes, if these elements are present in your story, it becomes easier to incorporate different elements of body language. Having said that, you can incorporate elements of body language into just about any speech. I have realized that the elements of body language are not just good to have; they are must-haves for any speech. Why? The audience will not trust you if your body language does not complement your words.

For this project, more effort should be spent on the *delivery*.

## SPEECH SCRIPT and ANALYSIS (in bold):

*Title*: Day out with friends

**Opening is a Story. I am orienting the audience to the scene.**

I was lazing in my bed when I heard, "'Wake up. It is already 8 o'clock."

**Please note the use of alliterations. The 'L' sound in 'lazing in a lounge room in Lake View Resort in Lonavala' forms the alliteration. I became a big fan of alliterations after project 4 and I started using them as much as possible.**

Mr. Toastmaster, fellow Toastmasters, and dear guests, on Sept. 21, 2009, I was lazing in a lounge room at Lake View Resort in Lonavala, India. As none of our friends woke up, my friend Shakti was bellowing at us, "Lazy laggards, why did we come to Lonavala?" Vijay, another companion on our trip, quipped, "To booze." Please do not judge me from Vijay's words. Actually, I am a teetotaler except for a few pegs of cocktails at social gatherings. Back at the scene there, all our other friends were still slumbering.

**There was movement around the stage in the following instances: a) action of splashing water, b) friends running helter-skelter, c) Dinesh coming stealthily and pouring it over Shakti.**

In a while Shakti carried in an orange bucket full of water and started splashing us. Seeing this, everyone sprang from the bed and ran helter-skelter. Dinesh, the chubbiest guy among us, stealthily managed a bucketful of water and emptied it over Shakti. It did not take us long. We guys had successfully converted the Lake View Resort's lounge room into an actual lake. Within an hour, we got ready in casual outfits. Luckily, we had a silver-colored Corolla and all of us sat comfortably in it.

**Saying the below emotion helped the audience to empathize with my situation. This helps bring out the natural facial expressions**

Unluckily, the chauffeur appeared to be in some kind of hurry, and at one point, we doubted what was racing faster, the car or our hearts! Soon the Corolla came to a grinding halt at Mulshi Dam and we jumped out relieved that we were alive!

**Please note the use of triad (see italics). Triad is a concept where you present ideas as a group of three (3 words, 3 sentences, 3 paragraphs). Always remember that ideas presented using triad will be easily remembered.**

On our way to the dam, *the rain gods blessed us with a heavy downpour, cool mist engulfed us in its arms, and wet earth scented us with its aroma.* Suddenly, Shakti exclaimed, 'Wow!!! Look at that." In that direction, we witnessed a spectacular waterfall. I instigated my friends to trek up the acclivity and feast our eyes upon the spectacle. During our ascent, we encountered a stream. This stream originated from the base of the waterfall and merged into the dam.

**I show the movement through bushes and woods. Observe that the sentence has the use of triad and alliteration (damp, dark, dangerous). *Secret*: The use of triads and alliteration will make your speech beautiful. Another secret: Try combining different methods and techniques. You'll create something beautiful. The audience should not feel you used a technique or a method when they hear you. They should say, "This is amazing!"**

Eager enough, we cut across the stream and then overcame damp bushes, dark woods, and dangerous reptiles to reach the waterfall. The beauty and splendor of the thunderous waterfall from the chasm of the Western Ghats along with the lush green background left us speechless. At that location, my friend Vijay enthused, "Come on, guys. Let us click a photo... OK, you all move out. I need a solo photograph." It is fine to click photographs; even I took some. But my friends were clicking photos as if Yash Chopra and Mani Ratnam were desperate to see our album.

**I show facial expression that shows astonishment (Tip: Try different expressions during practice and see which fits well) or amusement at what my friends were doing.**

After the photo shoot, we headed back.

**I show contrast (gentle vs. violent) through left and right-hand gestures.**

We were astonished to see the gentle stream turn into a violent river because of the continuous rainfall. The flow was so fierce that if we let ourselves loose inside the stream, we would have a free roller-coaster ride into the dam.

**In the below para, I enacted Shankar and his body language for showing the movement along the chain, slowly and steadily.**

Shankar laid out his strategy, "We will form a chain and cross the stream sideways. I will go first and then the rest will follow." Everyone agreed. Shankar was the lead followed by Murali, Naveen, Vijay, Shakti, Dinesh, and finally myself. I held Dinesh's left hand with my right. The chain began to move slowly and steadily.

Everyone was nervous but stayed calm.

**I used the following movements: Excited action when Shankar screams; role-play Dinesh and extend hands to show that someone is suspended.**

All of a sudden, Dinesh slipped. I clutched Dinesh's left hand. On the other side, Shakti clasped Dinesh's right hand. Shankar screamed, "Do not move, guys. Stay where you are."

**During the below, I show movement through pulling action.**

Dinesh was suspended between Shakti and me for 2 minutes. Nevertheless, we pulled him up against the force of water. But the future is unpredictable, and at any moment the savior might become the one who has to be saved.

**And then, I show movement through slipping action.**

The moment Dinesh got his footing back, I lost mine. I went down heavily into the rushing water. Cold water gushed into my ears, nostrils, mouth, and fogged my glasses. Four of my sensory perceptions were malfunctioning and with the last remaining one, I could feel the force of swirling water on my body. The icy hands of fear gripped my heart.

**I do movement for doing dad's role play.**

Without *rhyme or reason*, my dad's 10-year-old advice flashed before my mind. "Rama, learn swimming. It will come in handy one day." Back then I had scoffed and did not heed his suggestion. Now, in the middle of a torrential flow of *water, without a firm footing*, I regretted having scoffed at my dad. Despite my *brain being* overloaded, it somehow managed to give the *right instructions to my right hand.*

**I do some drama by clasping and dragging.**

I firmly clasped Dinesh's left hand. Through the foggy glasses, I saw the chain begin to move *steadily towards the safety of the shore.*

**I show a sense of relief after reaching the shore through a "phew" gesture.**

I sensed them dragging me against the force of water. Finally, we reached terra firma. I experienced the bliss of my life.

**During the conclusion, showed a numb face when saying the danger of death, had a proud expression and clasped hands gesture to show friendship, perseverance and unity.**

For the first time in my life, I faced the *danger of death*. I stayed on the jaws of death for 10 long minutes. Had I let go of Dinesh's hand I could not imagine what would have happened. My friends did not fail me against forces of *danger, desperation, and death*. Instead, they put forth a perfect example of the true spirit of *friendship, perseverance, and unity*.

## TECHNIQUES FOR DELIVERY:

As I said earlier, the focus of this project is on delivery. Repeat the exercise of looking at your speech video and working on the distracting mechanisms. Use techniques from earlier projects, and then work on incorporating the following methods related to different elements of body language.

1. *Stance*: This is the first element to be focused on. Just stand straight with a straight back (this changed my game of speaking), keep your hands to the side with your fingers slightly curled, and start talking.

2. *Movement*: Have you seen people moving from side to side without any purpose? I have read numerous articles, and heard from champions, and one thing that stands out is: Never move without purpose. Let me explain. *Move only*

*when you want to communicate some idea.* For example, moving sideways or diagonally sideways to the back of the room can indicate you are going back in time. Taking a step backward from the audience can indicate a weak moment; a step forward can indicate a strong moment. Moving to the left part of the stage is considered a weak position to convey any point, moving to the right part of the stage is a power position. These are all what I learned, observed, and applied. A word of caveat: they might not apply always. Please be a good judge of your speech and use them wisely.

3. *Facial Expressions*: This is an area we do not focus on while preparing our speech. Why do I say this? Record yourself and see your speech. Do you have natural facial expressions that agree with what you say? If the answer is "No", then your focus is internal. The best speeches are the ones that have an external focus. You can orchestrate different expressions for each sentence of the speech. This might help but it'll be hard for you to sequence and be natural. There is a simpler technique. Get your speech script in your muscle memory, then allow the emotions to flow. Feel the emotions in your heart, and practice your speech. Trust yourself. When you do this, you will have natural facial expressions and your speech will become smooth and beautiful.

4. *Gestures*: Now, let's talk about gestures. Hands are the main tools of communication for gesturing. Please follow the practical tips below while gesturing.
a. Keep your fingers straight or slightly curled.
b. Check if your hands move from elbow level or shoulder level. Remember, your hands should move from shoulder

level. (I was ignoring this for a long time and I learnt this from

c. Do not point at the audience.

d. Use open-palm gestures to build trust with your audience.

e. Hands should stroke at the right word. Stroking before or after the intended word will seem artificial and distracting. The moment someone feels that the gestures seem to be planted, they won't trust you. Even though you can have deliberate gestures, they should seem natural and fluid.

f. Once your script is in your muscle memory, rehearse your speech with energy. Observe how your hands move. Note the gestures that add emphasis to your speech and note the distracting movements. Then, work to stop the distracting movements and let your fluid gestures do the magic.

g. You should also be comfortable keeping your hands to your side. Not gesturing also can add impact to certain parts of the speech. You have to make the call.

5. *Eye Contact*: This helps to establish a connection with your audience. To have seamless eye contact is challenging. I used to glaze over my audience. This might be OK till your project 4 but in this project, you have to go to the next level. Practice it this way. Divide your audience into quadrants. Imagine talking to one person looking directly into their eye for 5 seconds in the first quadrant; then move on gradually to the other person in the audience in the next quadrant (don't move on to the next immediate person); then move on to another person gradually in the third quadrant and so on. Remember to talk with that one person for that whole sentence or idea. Repeat the whole cycle but with different people. If you are successful in doing this, your eye contact will create

a great connection. And I bet you will be considered far more credible and authentic.

**One last thing:** Trying to incorporate all the above techniques might be overwhelming. In that case, first, get your speech script in your muscle memory. Having your script in muscle memory means knowing your speech so well that you can say the script even if I were to wake you up in the middle of the night. Here's the thing: Once you know the script thoroughly, different elements of body language will seem to gel smoothly and naturally.

Please don't forget to:

1. Practice, Practice, Practice.

2. Record your speech when you deliver your project before the audience.

# Chapter Six

# Vocal Variety

At the end of the day, what is our goal?

Become a better speaker? Overcome stage fright? Speak with confidence?

And who is the real driver for this?

Your voice!

Even if you have the perfect speech script and perfect body language, if you do not have vocal variety, your speech will lose its sheen.

Can you imagine the criticality of this particular element of public speaking?

Let us see the speech objectives:

a. Use voice volume, pitch, rate, and quality to reflect and add meaning and interest to your message.

b. Use pauses to enhance your message.

c. Use vocal variety smoothly and naturally.

From objectives, it's obvious that you need to learn to use your voice for effective speaking. To do that, we need to create a scope to use different elements of vocal variety in this project. How do we achieve this? We can accomplish this by having characters say **dialogue**, incorporating **humor**, building strong **emotion,** and creating **suspense**. To incorporate these elements, you need to use your voice effectively. For my project, I selected a story where the emotional connection in the story was powerful. Since I was personally interested in learning humor, I learned it on the side and incorporated it as well.

The delivery aspect of this project needs more attention. So it would be prudent to spend time on delivery. Please note that all the skills and experience of previous projects need to be incorporated into the current project as you progress through your speech projects. This is important.

## SPEECH SCRIPT & ANALYSIS (in bold):

Before we check the script and analysis, let's quickly talk about *pauses,* one of the most powerful elements in vocal variety. Pauses have been marked as <s p> (short pause) or <p> (normal pause). Even though I had humor in earlier projects, I was waiting to highlight the mechanics because pauses play a major role in creating humor. Tip: Rule of 3 can be the easiest tool for a beginner to start using humor. The formula is say something *Expected*, say something *Expected*, and say something *Unexpected*. You'll see the application in the speech example shared below.

*Title*: Three Doors

**Opening as usual was a story that stretched for a good one minute. I purposely did this to involve my audience in my speech.**

This January, my manager put me in charge of a critical project. Being a fairly ambitious guy, I worked day in and day out to get that most awaited promotion. I was exhausted. A few weeks ago, at 5 in the morning, the phone jangled me awake.

**The tone used: high pitch and exaggeration when mentioning "third girlfriend."**

**And also, observe the Rule of 3. "Third time," "3 months,", "third girlfriend" (unexpected)**

As soon as I picked up the call, I heard, "Why didn't you call me? Don't you remember I exist? Do you love me?" These questions were fired for the third time in the past 3 months by my <s p> third girlfriend. <p> I am just kidding; <p> by my one and only girlfriend, Lavanya.

**Setting context about the topic: giving my opinion about relationships.**

Fellow Toastmasters and guests, relationships are hard, and the ones with people we truly love can be particularly hard. But at that point, all I wanted was some sleep!

Exhausted, I fell back asleep but not completely. I was half awake and half asleep. In that state, I felt some part of me was out of my body.

**Transition: From me to you.**

Have you been there? <p> I was in such a situation for the third time in the past 3 months.

**This speech was constructed like a movie: Please observe fiction, dialogues, and humor. Use of normal pitch and tone.**

Some part of me cried for help. And every time it did, I saw 3 doors with a note on them that read, "Listen when you open the door."

**Use emotions to fuel your voice. I had an excited tone when I said, "The first time I chose door 1."**

The first time I chose door 1. Why? Well, I had to choose <p> some door. Inside door 1, I saw a movie being screened. I saw glimpses of my life situation where things went my way. <p> Everybody listened to me! <p> My ego loved it. I got excited instantly, feeling how great I was and how fortunate Lavanya was to have me as her boyfriend.

**Have frustration and an egoistic attitude in the tone. Played the character of Lavanya and snapped back. (Paused before "idiot" to create humor.) Used an Angry tone for "idiot." When a girl gets angry and says something like this, people laugh!**

I called Lavanya and said, "Don't you know how hard I am working? Don't you know how important my role is?"

Lavanya said, "Yes, I know how important you are, <p> idiot."<p>

What?

I didn't expect that. We had what we call a <p> high-volume discussion. My relationship was not working.

The second time I chose door 2 because door 1 was not working. Inside door 2, I saw another movie being screened. Guess who was in the movie? <p> It was me again. I saw my life situations where I apologized for running out of the situation.

**Use of low volume and pitch. Almost apologetic.**

I picked up my phone and said, "Lavanya, I am sorry. Please don't make this an issue."

I was sure that Lavanya would feel better.

**Use of a high and aggressive tone.**

Lavanya said, 'I, I am making an issue. What do you think, Rama? You say sorry and I will <s p> forgive you?"

**Use of a sarcastic tone. I had an attitude of a loser. The goal was to create empathy.**

Now, I really felt like an <p> idiot <p>. We had a low-volume discussion. <p> This was worse. My relationship was still not working.

**For these lines, "The third time...Listen," I used an assertive tone. In the following sentence, I stressed the word "listened" and soothingly finished the sentence.**

The third time, I didn't want Rama's ego in door 1. I didn't want Rama's apology in door 2. I wanted a better outcome. I entered door 3. Inside door 3, <p> no movie was being screened. Now, I chose to <pp> listen.

**This was told in a sincere and low tone. I got very good reviews for this dialogue.**

When I called Lavanya, I listened to her anger, I listened to her hurt, but then I heard <p> something beautiful, for what we could be. I said: <p> "You are missing me, right? It feels so great to hear your voice, honey." I sensed solemn silence. I melted, and so did Lavanya. I heard something beautiful.

**This was uttered as if Lavanya melted.**

She said, "Yes, I missed you badly, <p> stupid." <p> Through the narrow telephone line, we found a connection.

**Use of loud and clear voice to talk to the audience.**

Friends, what am I really saying here?

**Conclusion: I said this as sincerely as possible. I think by being sincere, we become authentic and credible as a speaker. I used pauses to add humor or make an impact. The last pause (denoted as <PPP>) was for 5 seconds. I wanted each audience member to think of someone important in his or her life.**

<p> Our connections with our loved ones are not about ego or apology but about listening. Relationships will blossom because <p> Love Listens.

I'd like to leave you with a question the most precious people in your life might be asking of you. The question is not, how much do you love them? The question is:

*Are you <PPP> listening?*


## TECHNIQUES FOR DELIVERY:

Repeat the exercise of working on the distracting mechanisms of your earlier project. After that, use techniques from the earlier projects. Then focus on incorporating the techniques given below. I bet you will grow by leaps and bounds.

1. How to sound clear: Complete every word and give space before you go to the next word. *Make sure you end the words properly.* This might be hard or weird to practice but I guar-

antee you that this will have a lot of impact on your speech. Have you heard songs or music from a high-end sound system (heard of BOSE speakers)? Your speech's sound should be in that fashion.

2. How to find your optimum tone: First, practice in a tone that you speak to a friend. Once you are comfortable, practice in a louder tone. Once you are comfortable in a louder tone, practice it in a softer tone. By doing this, you will free any vocal blocks and arrive at an optimum tone that will seem natural and vibrant. When you do the above exercise, volume, rate, and pitch will fall into place.

3. How to control the pace of the speech: Practice till you have your speech in your muscle memory. If you don't have your speech in the muscle memory, it might be hard for you to play with the vocal variety of the speech. At least, it used to be hard for me. Once the speech is in your muscle memory, you can control the pace and use intonation, exaggeration, etc., for different words in your speech.

4. How to have a strong audience connect: Even though you might have done this unconsciously, let us make it deliberate. *Add emotion to your speech.* How do you do this? Tell the audience how you feel about what you are saying. *Feel the emotion in your heart.* If your content should make your audience feel happy, you should also feel happiness. If your content should make the audience feel sad, you should also feel sadness. *Be clear on the emotional intent of your speech.* Hollywood actors do this, why not you?

Please don't forget to:

1. Practice, Practice, Practice.

2. Record your speech when you deliver your project before the audience.

# Chapter Seven

# Research your Topic

So far, we completed the projects to hone different building blocks of a speech. And now, it's time to apply them.

Did it occur to you that *Research your Topic* means the presentation of a white paper after years of research? If you did, please join my advanced abstract club!

Let us see the objectives of this speech:

a. Collect information about your topic from numerous sources.

b. Carefully support your points and opinions with specific facts, examples, and illustrations gathered through research.

I got my topic idea when my co-volunteer at Connecting (a non-governmental organization for suicide prevention in Pune, India) was talking about the production of alcohol from food grains. I was also looking for a speech topic and it worked out for me. I've mentioned it earlier, please do not spend too much selecting a topic. Go through Chapter 11, an excerpt from my book Public Speaking Topic Secrets, and see if it sparks an idea or two on how to select your topic.

Here is a project that will force you to research and then present it. Let me break it down so that you don't have to do research from Harvard, Stanford, or nature journals to prove your point. Till now, your speeches are *your* opinions but now you will research what is "out there." All you have to do is know what others have found out about your topic, know what they feel about your topic, and present it correctly. You are required to cite *different* sources to substantiate your speech.

Please keep in mind; that your speech should have all the elements that you have learned in earlier projects.

## SPEECH SCRIPT & ANALYSIS (in bold):

*Title*: Alcohol and Food

**Yes, you noticed that I changed my opening style. It was not a story. Rather it was the headline in a leading newspaper in India.**

"Bombay High Court dismisses Public Interest Litigation against the government subsidies for food grain-based distilleries"

Mr. Toastmaster, fellow Toastmasters, and dear guests, this headline in *Indian Express* perturbed me.

**In transition into the topic; I am using a rhetorical question (It's a tool to engage the audience. You don't expect the audience to answer the question) as the tool.**

"How can the government give a subsidy to produce alcohol from food grains?"

I got curious to know the amount of subsidy given to these distilleries.

**I am citing an article in a leading daily newspaper that gives a big number for an argument that supports my motive (that the government is not doing the right thing). I also add my dimension to the story and transition to the next point to nullify the government's explanation.**

From an article in *Hindustan Times*, I found that the government is all set to release a staggering 5000 Cr (a billion dollars) order to reduce one-third of the cost of liquor production. Now, I got curious to know about the government's explanation to support this move. The government's first point was that there is adequate food supply in Maharashtra, so diverting large quantities of food grains to alcohol manufacturers would not affect food security within the state. People easily fool me, not because I am a software engineer but because I am poor in facts and figures. So I wanted to check the food situation in Maharashtra.

I am going to marinate you with a little bit of data.

**Citing facts from an international organization to prove a point.**

The research findings of the International Food Policy Research Institute (IFPRI) showed a different picture altogether. Maharashtra scored 23-29 in the ISHI (India State Hunger Index). And unfortunately, this score means that food security falls under the Alarming Category.

**Numbers from a major newspaper publication.**

According to the Economic Survey of Maharashtra, in 2005-06, the cereal production of Maharashtra was 97.46

lakh tons whereas in the same year, the consumption was 122.8 lakh tons which means Maharashtra imported 25.34 lakh tons of cereals. The demand for food grains for these new distilleries is 13.13 lakh tons per annum.

**I am translating those mind-boggling numbers to a base figure of 100 so that we can relate to the same.**

What is it that we understand from all these facts? Out of 100 people, food for 20 people is imported. But according to IFPRI, out of 100 people, 26 stay hungry. With this current status, our state Maharashtra is ready to divert more food grains, and that too for the manufacture of alcohol. How ridiculous is this?

The government's second point was that the distilleries would pay a higher and regular income to farmers and that would avoid farmers' suicide. This fact was not at all convincing.

Yes, a small percentage of farmers who sell their produce to the factory will profit. But for the vast majority of farmers of Maharashtra and other poor people, rising alcohol addiction because of these distilleries would increase their poverty and problems.

**Here, I am using an interesting finding spearheaded by a famous figure in India to support my point.**

The proof of this fact is the statement of our president, Pratibha Patil. When she was the social welfare minister, her officials were asked to find the usage of additional income from the Employment Guarantee Scheme. The findings were an eye-opener: 50% squandered their money on liquor and gambling. Besides, as food grains will be diverted towards alcohol, food will become more expensive. Thus, with an increase in poverty and hunger, suicides are bound to increase and not decrease.

The government's third reason was that it wanted to promote grain-based alcohol to meet the need for potable alcohol. This claim just floors me. The government is more concerned about the future availability of alcohol for the public rather than checking for food security in the state. The irony here is that it is using food grains to produce alcohol!!!

**After researching the three reasons for the government's move and mentioning the facts to oppose it, I am mentioning a finding from WHO.**

According to the World Health Organization (WHO), the number of alcohol addicts in a society is proportional to the availability of alcohol.

**To convince the audience against the government's move, I am citing some results based on research.**

A renowned scientist, Sully Ledermann, has proven that when the consumption of alcohol increases in a society, the prevalence of adverse consequences of alcohol in that society increases in geometric proportion. In a developing country like India where the purchasing power is increasing, a large proportion of the benefits of development would get squandered over alcohol.

**Citing an example to prove the ill effects of alcohol regulation.**

The example of Thailand is in front of us: In recent decades, government controls on production were removed and taxes were not in place to obstruct the growth of the alcohol market. Historically, Thailand had a low usage of alcohol because of the influence of Buddhism. However recent surveys show that around one-third of their population has now started to drink, and 22.7% of Thai drinkers have alcohol use disorders!

Yes, I can understand and appreciate all this data but aren't these things common? This is the first response some might get. Why? Because we are used to it. Friends, can't we see the implications of this move? Whose money is the government giving as a subsidy? It is our tax money. Tomorrow, a 20-buck pizza might cost 30 bucks. A 10-buck item might cost 20 bucks. Is there anyone doing something about this?

**Coming up with a solution rather than just giving a talk.**

Yes, there is a group called NIRMAN. They have filed Public Interest Litigation in the Supreme Court against the government. I showed my support by signing in this form to support NIRMAN. The slow progress in justice of societal issues is not because of the violence of the bad, but because of the silence of good.

**As a conclusion, I am giving a solution and a simple call for action so that the folks feel satisfied that they did something to support this move.**

Let's support this selfless group by signing this sheet and sending our message to the government that we do not agree to open these unreasonable distilleries.


**TECHNIQUES FOR DELIVERY:**

Check the recording of your previous project delivery. Repeat the exercise of working on the distracting mechanisms. For this project onwards, refer to Chapter 12, for the consolidated delivery checklist. Please don't forget to:

1. Practice, Practice, Practice.

2. Record your speech when you deliver your project before the audience.

# Chapter Eight

# Use of Visual Aids

Visual aids can convey your message in less time and create more impact. A picture is worth a thousand words. This project is about the usage of visual aids.

Have you seen presentations with a PowerPoint, or some props: a book, pen, card, or charts? If you did, then you have experienced the use of visual aids.

Let us see the objectives of this speech:

a. Select visual aids that are appropriate for your message and the audience.

b. Use visual aids correctly with ease and confidence.

I have given an excerpt from my book Public Speaking Topic Secrets in chapter 11. I hope this sparks an idea or two. However, let's see some specific ideas to expand your perception of using visual aids for a speech.

1. A speech that involves describing a practical problem and proposing a solution. Example: There is a parking problem. You need visual aids like PowerPoint to showcase the problem (current location, area, and figures) and also to show the solution (new location, etc.).

2. How to create a _ _ _ _ _ (e.g., website, video). Use of PowerPoint, and flip charts to show the critical steps in the process.

3. A speech topic about your loved ones where you can use props to depict the person or characters. For example, Randy Harvey, 2004 World Champion of Public Speaking, in his "Lessons from Fat Dad" speech used "chair" as a prop to depict his car and used the same chair to depict his father sitting on the chair.

4. Find a key item that made an impact in your life. Try to build a speech around it so that the key item can be used as a prop in your speech. For example, Lance Miller used a parking ticket in his speech. It was an important turning point story in his 2005 Winning Speech "The Ultimate Question" (worth watching!). To cite another example, Vikas Jhingran used an admit letter that he received from a college in his 2007 World Championship Speech "The Swami's Question." I hope the above examples help you expand your perception of using visual aids.

Visual aids are not limited to PowerPoint. I did not want to use PowerPoint. Visual aids for my speech were:

1. A cup with shattered plastic pieces
2. A tennis ball
3. A knife and a whetstone

## SPEECH SCRIPT & ANALYSIS (in bold):

*Title*: Tormentor

I am a born speaker! An excellent orator!

Fellow Toastmasters and dear guests, I was wrong. It all started with my first project. I wrote my Ice Breaker with all my enthusiasm and proudly sent it to my first mentor. I felt so happy that I had created such a nice Ice Breaker script. But when I opened my reviewed speech using Microsoft Word, the number of words in the comments exceeded the number of words of my speech.

**I had a cup with plastic pieces and I threw it up. It fell and the pieces were scattered.**

At that time my confidence level in writing speeches shattered like this.

I realized the untold truth that our script looks splendid only to us and not necessarily to others.

After my Ice Breaker, a shuffle between tormentors, I mean mentors and mentees happened. Now I got assigned not to a normal tormentor but a super tormentor. Every time I sent a script for review, a reply would come.

"Dear Rama, a very well-written speech. However, I felt that the opening was not that great. The conclusion could have been powerful, and the structure was not supported that well."

After reading those comments, I am pretty sure not only I but also you would have felt like replying, "Dear Mentor, then why in the world did you write – 'a very well-written speech'?" Instead, I replied, "Dear Mentor, I appreciate the constructive comments you gave me. Please find the reworked script." For that particular project, I sent my script 10 times before my mentor finalized it.

**I used a tennis ball and bounced it back and forth to show review and rework concepts.**

My script was like this ball bouncing back and forth between my mentor and me.

Review

Rework

Review rework

Review rework.

I had a notion that Toastmasters were a crazy world calling speeches as projects. Only when I ended up doing the rework an umpteen number of times did I realize that writing quality code for a software project was much easier than writing a quality speech for a Toastmasters project.

Once you complete your speech writing, if you feel that the project is over, then I have to say in comprehensible terms, "Only Build is over. Testing is remaining." And yes, this testing is your delivery part where the mentor gives the final touch to your speech... I say, "Mr. Toastmaster, fellow Toastmasters, and dear guests."

He goes, "Wait, wait... Give pause; give pause. Say 'Mr. Toastmaster, fellow Toastmasters, and dear guests.'"

I say, "Lavanya, you are missing me, huh?"

My mentor says, "Damn...put some feeling into it. Say 'Lavanya, you are missing me, huh.'"

After almost 10 to 12 reviews and 5 to 6 delivery practice sessions, I wondered, where am I heading?

**I had a knife and a whetstone and showed how the knife is sharpened. This added more impact to my message.**

But it was only when I won my first Area Level Best Pre-pared Speaker award that I realized that I was wrong when I thought that my speech was like this ball and my mentor was like a wall. Rather, my speech was like this knife, and my mentor was like this stone making my speech sharper and sharper with every review.

As I progressed with my other speeches, my perception of mentoring and the mentor changed. The tormentor became the guarantor that my speech would be a success. At one point, I became the tormentee. Can you imagine in the 14th version of my script, I am sending an e-mail:

Dear Mentor,

I am very grateful that my speech has come this far. But still, I could see a lot of possibilities to improve the opening. Can you please suggest a better idea?

Do you all like public speaking? Do you all want to have fun? Do you want to become a great speaker? Listen to this. Darren LaCroix, World Champion of Public Speaking in 2001, had a writing coach as well as a speaking coach. He still gets mentored and is a strong advocate of mentoring. If he can still have writing and speaking mentors, I am sure we all can understand the importance of mentoring.

Friends, each one present here has the innate ability to write and deliver a good speech. But only mentoring can make your good speech into a great speech.

## TECHNIQUES FOR DELIVERY:

Check the recording of your previous project delivery. Repeat the exercise of working on the distracting mechanisms. Refer to Chapter 12, for a consolidated delivery checklist.

For this specific project, take care that the audience members do not know about your props beforehand. For my speech, I placed the props behind the lectern. I took the props only when my speech needed it and gracefully placed them back to avoid distraction. *Surprise is one of the most important traits that need to be maintained in a speech.* If you observe any great movie or play, the thing that keeps the audience hooked is the surprise element. It is a major engagement device. So try to have visual aids that surprise the audience and are also relevant to your message.

Now, let us understand the usage of some specific visual aids.

*Flip Charts*: I recommend flip charts if you are planning on giving an informational speech. It will seem as if you are creating an idea as you deliver your speech.

*PowerPoint*: As a speaker, you need to get comfortable with PowerPoint. I think it is one of the most wrongly used visual aids. Just keep the below points in mind.

1. Do not write more than 6 words in a bullet point.

2. Do not have more than 3 or 4 bullets in a slide.

3. Make sure your words are clear and legible.

4. Have a minimum number of slides.

5. You should be able to speak even if you don't have a PowerPoint.

6. Don't turn your back and look at the slides when you are explaining the content.

7. If possible, get a remote control for navigating through your slides.

8. Have blank slides (full black) between the slides. When you do this, the audience will again start focusing on you.

Please don't forget to:

1. Practice, Practice, Practice.

2. Record your speech when you deliver your project before the audience.

# Chapter Nine

# Persuade with Power

Well, well, well, if you have reached here after completing the earlier speeches, I will take a pause. Pat yourself on your back for a job well done. You are awesome. You deserve the appreciation for the work and the effort. In this project and the next project, we will focus more on the impact rather than the mechanics.

Let us see the objectives of this speech:

a. Persuade the audience to adopt your viewpoint or ideas or to take some action.

b. Appeal to the audience's interests.

c. Use logic and emotion to support your position.

d. Avoid using notes.

I have given an excerpt from my book Public Speaking Topic Secrets in chapter 11. Please refer to the section on persuasive speech topics. This will help you to find your perfect topic.

My mentor Jerry Aiyathurai (finalist in World Championship) asked me to answer:

1. Who are you?

2. What is it all about?

3. What is your message about it?

His words struck a chord with me. If you apply this simple exercise, you can create a powerful persuasive speech.

Mark Brown, 1995 Champion of Public Speaking, said, "Your life tells a story and there is someone out there who needs to hear it." Someone said, "If your life was a book and you were the author, how would you like the story to be?"

This is the beauty of giving persuasive speeches. You will undergo a journey, which did not exist earlier. You will be compelled to think beyond. Stories, especially personal ones form the crux of persuasive speeches.

If you want to learn more persuasive speeches, please check out my book *Connect Using Humor and Story*, where I show how to combine principles of humor, and story to create persuasive speeches.


## SPEECH SCRIPT & ANALYSIS (in bold):

*Title*: Does anyone need help?

**The opening is a personal experience to grab the audience's attention**

A few weeks ago, I asked my friend Siddique, "Why do you look so tired?"

Through his dark brown-color framed spectacles, Siddique looked into my eyes and gave a wry smile.

**I am stating the problem or the need of the hour.**

Mr. Toastmaster, fellow Toastmasters, and dear guests, I sensed that Siddique was deeply disturbed and emotionally down. I paused for a while. I asked, "Siddique, what is bothering you right now?" Siddique said, "Nothing, Rama."

Later in the evening, I had to take another friend to a movie. Meanwhile, Siddique requested my company that day. At his home, with my legs crossed, I comfortably sat on the maroon couch while Siddique sat on his bed.

**I am involving the audience to empathize with the situation.**

Suddenly, Siddique turned out and said, "Rama, I am feeling awful. I want to tell you something."

Meanwhile, I got a call from my friend to go to the movie.

**I am asking a rhetorical question to drive my point.**

Now how would you respond to this situation? He was in a clear state of distress.

**Coming up with a reason why I am positioned to give a solution.**

If you say that you have to leave in 10 minutes to watch a movie, would Siddique continue?

Of course not. Am I an expert in this field? No, but I had been volunteering for Connecting, an NGO for people who feel distressed and suicidal. I learned that if people are disturbed or distressed, we need to give them space to speak.

I postponed my plan and stayed with Siddique. After taking his own time, Siddique said, "I broke up with my girlfriend." What should I do now? What about saying, "Can you check for someone else?" If it had been 3 months ago, I would have asked that question. However, my perception changed after the training I received from the great mentors at Connecting.

**Presenting the solution.**

They taught me that first, I have to be the listener and not the adviser.

**Asking rhetorical questions to rule out the questions that the audience might have.**

You might ask, why don't you suggest how to win his girlfriend back? If you give someone a solution, it is based on your value system and not his. So you should not give him a solution. Who is the only person who can decide which would be the right solution? It is the disturbed person himself.

**Building upon the solution of listening to others.**

Back at Siddique's home, I applied this principle by asking Siddique, "Can you please tell me more?" I let him speak more and more till the point where he didn't have anything left to share. You see, your mere presence would create wonders more than the words you say to them.

If I am telling you not to ask specific details, not give solutions, not sympathize, then I can hear you mumble, is this guy telling us to be dumb? No, you should not be dumb because you are the torch who would be helping them find their light.

**I am elaborating more on the solution of listening.**

They just need that support and you would be that invaluable support at that moment.

Let me ask you a question. According to you what is the one thing which characterizes the state of distress? It is the feelings. Your focus is to probe their feelings such as anger, love, loneliness, sadness, or anxiousness. You just need to help them and let them vent out these feelings through words.

**Presenting the exact solution to the problem.**

My coaches have told me that the most important thing that you should do is to give them emotional support. I stayed with Siddique for 2 hours listening to him till he felt comfortable.

**Explaining the benefits of the solution.**

If each one of you starts giving emotional support to your friends, family, or your co-workers, or any acquaintances that you know, you will be a part of the change, that this world needs.

**I am helping the audience visualize the benefit of having implemented this solution.**

At the end of the day, before you sleep, if you feel that you have done a selfless act by empowering somebody else to get going in his or her life, the satisfaction you would get would feel like magic.

**A clear call to action by using a suitable metaphor in the speech.**

The next time when you come across a situation, like mine, prove to yourself that you can be the torch to shed light in someone's life.


## TECHNIQUES FOR DELIVERY:

Check the recording of your previous project delivery. Repeat the exercise of working on the distracting mechanisms. Refer to Chapter 12, for a consolidated delivery checklist.

*An honest and sincere speech can beat a made-up sensational speech.* I am telling this from experience. Please trust me on this. Practice as if you are having a one-to-one heartfelt conversation with a close friend. Are you fully convinced with your viewpoint? Show your stand to the audience. *Your conviction must radiate when you are giving a persuasive speech.*

Please don't forget to:

1. Practice, Practice, Practice.

2. Record your speech when you deliver your project before the audience.

# Chapter Ten

# Inspire your Audience

How do you make your audience say, "Awesome"? Let's say someone asked me, "What gift would you like to have as a speaker?" I would reply, "The gift of inspiring my audience."

Do you realize that just by using words, you can influence someone's life? Think about it. It is powerful stuff.

Let us see the objectives:

a. To inspire the audience by appealing to noble motives and challenging the audience to achieve a higher level of beliefs or achievement.

b. To appeal to the audience's needs and emotions using stories, anecdotes, and quotes to add drama.

I still get excited about writing and delivering inspiring speeches. This is one of the most profound things you can do for yourself. You know what will happen if you do that? I can guarantee that at least one person will be inspired by your speech. And that person will be YOU. You will automatically follow your message because you have created it. I cannot explain this in words but you have to feel the thrill and excitement when you create an inspiring speech. Don't try shortcuts by copying someone else's speech that does not resonate with you. You would be fooling yourself and wasting your time.

After completing the *Persuade with Power* project, I started to understand the real meaning of passion. I enjoyed spending time honing my speeches. The best part was I never felt that I was enduring. I was enjoying it. Bing! I got the idea, Pursue Your Passion.

When do you get inspired? That is a very important question to ask. Don't you get inspired when you "feel" a speech? Why is it going to be different for your audience? And when would they "feel" your speech? They will feel if *your* story resonates with *their* story. And I believe that personal stories are the best tools to create inspiring speeches. Don't think that you don't have anything to say because you didn't climb Mt. Everest, fight in a world war, or save a dying person. Someone had said that if you reach adulthood, you have enough stories to share than you ever thought. In the documentary movie SPEAK (a must-watch movie for public speaking enthusiasts), Mark Brown, 1995 World Champion of Public Speaking, said, "Your life tells a story, and there is someone out there who needs to hear it." This is a profound statement that can generate a lot of ideas for you. You have already explored topics in the earlier project, but instead of persuading your audience to agree with your viewpoint, your core focus is to inspire them to new possibilities.

I have given an excerpt from my book Public Speaking Topic Secrets in chapter 11. Please refer to the section on inspiring speech topics. It can help you find a topic.

**SPEECH SCRIPT & ANALYSIS (in bold):**

*Title*: What's drives you?

**Starting with my favorite opening style, a story.**

On Oct. 1, 1993, in a packed auditorium, I walked onto the stage wearing a blue half-trouser and white half-sleeve shirt. I held the mike and started a speech: "Time is a gift given by God and one has to use it wisely…" That was my first public speaking experience. I bombed. It was painful. I wanted to learn this art. So I volunteered for every stage appearance. And then I started to get comfortable on stage. Even though I developed a passion for public speaking, I ignored it as I grew up.

Madame Toastmaster, fellow Toastmasters, and dear guests, I ignored something I loved to do.

**Transition to the audience and give them time to reflect on the topic. There was a long pause to amplify the effect.**

Are you ignoring something that you love to do?

Time flew faster than light. I focused on academics completed my engineering and joined the corporate world as a software engineer. Even after I joined the corporate world I only pursued my assigned work and never pursued what I loved to do.

**Telling a specific incident to introduce the problem.**

Whenever I would see someone anchor on a stage, the child in me would say, "Rama – why are you not anchoring?"

But the big boy in me said, "There are greater things to pursue in life. Better focus on that, buddy."

**Building up the problem.**

I pursued my so-called greater things in life and did not listen to that innocent child asking me to pursue my passion.

**Taking the problem to an even higher level.**

In July 2008, my U.S. VISA to work at my client location was rejected. Almost everyone's visa in my friends' circle got approved. Although nobody had to be blamed, I was sad. There was a point when I would just stare at the computer monitor and only after an hour or so I would realize that I had not completed anything. I realized that I was enduring rather than enjoying my life

**Explaining the change that happened.**

In December 2008, I came across Toastmasters. I was fascinated by the whole idea and the enthusiasm shown by the members. At that point, I realized I never really boarded the train of my life.

**Reasoning out why I took action.**

I let the train pass me as if I was doing a favor to life. I wanted to change it. I joined Toastmasters. I was so delighted to see the amount of enthusiasm and inspiration I got while I worked on my speeches.

**Telling the benefits of taking action.**

My blood found new joy in circulation, my alertness levels touched new heights and each cell of my body displayed happiness. To be honest, I never really worked to get the best speaker award but worked to deliver a speech that was beneficial and enjoyable to my audience.

**Drama, excitement, and achievement are all woven into a story format.**

What I never expected were the awards that followed at various contests. I reached the District level humorous speech finals on my first attempt. When my manager heard about this, she brought it to the notice of my Senior Project Manager. After 15 minutes, I was called upon to my Delivery Manager's cabin. He said, "We have our Account town hall on the day after tomorrow and the IT heads of our client are visiting our unit. Can you host the event?" After a pause, he asked, "I have never seen you speak in public, would you be able to host this crucial event?" Before the big boy could analyze the situation, the child in me said, "Yes, I will do it." Everything seemed to have a connection. Out of nowhere, here I stood with an offer from my Delivery Manager to fulfill my desire. And maybe that was the reason the response came like a blitzkrieg. All things fell in place and there I stood behind the podium saying, "Ladies and gentlemen – welcome you all..." The event was a success and I received warm appreciation from my senior management.

**This is an important part of the speech where you are showing the results of the action that you have taken. Every problem-solution speech should have this part. The audience will trust you only if you show them the result.**

It seemed like magic. I fulfilled my desire without even having a plan. I believe the universe has only one purpose, to plant the right desires and help us fulfill them. It can help, but only if we pursue it with passion. The magic is pursuing your passion.

**I am using a quote by Ken Robinson (his TED talk is a must-watch) and conveying my specific purpose to inspire the audience to pursue their passion.**

I believe what Sir Ken Robinson said, "If you do something that resonates with your spirit, hours would seem like minutes, if you do something that does not resonate with your spirit, minutes would seem like hours." I am not telling you to quit your job tomorrow and do things you love. My point is you should give time to things you love. Maybe one day you will make a living out of it.

**In conclusion, leaving the audience with a sense of warmth and triggers so that they will find their passion.**

There are many things in life that would catch your eye but only some will catch your heart, and only a few would excite your spirit and energy. Find it and pursue it with passion.

## TECHNIQUES FOR DELIVERY:

Check the recording of your previous project delivery. Repeat the exercise of working on the distracting mechanisms. Refer to Chapter 12, for a consolidated delivery checklist.

Are you excited to take your final step in this journey? If you have come this far, you have already surpassed 90% of the people who want to improve their confidence and kill the fear of public speaking. This speech is the real deal. You have come a long way from where you started. If you look back, you will be amazed to see the distance you have covered. As I said earlier, if someone offers me a gift in the area of speaking, I would ask him or her for the gift of inspiring others. This is powerful stuff. You are going to own the stage to inspire others. Are you excited?

Let's do some groundwork before you take the stage. In one of his audio programs Darren LaCroix, 2001 World Champion of Public Speaking, said his mentor Mark Brown, 1995 World Champion of Public Speaking, told him:

*"Darren put your child or brother in the fourth row of your audience and give your speech so that he gets it."*

Who do you want to be a part of your audience? Think about it. How would your delivery change? Now your focus should shift from script and mechanics to connection and inspiration. See, techniques are just that. They are techniques. At the end of the day, the only question you should ask is, "Did my speech make an impact?"

Ask yourself:

· Why are you going to give this speech?

· What is your real purpose of standing in front of the audience?

· Would you inspire at least one of them?

These questions will clarify a lot of uncertainty. You should think about the audience and not about you. Craig Valentine, 1999 World Champion of Public Speaking, beautifully said, "I don't give speeches to get awarded or rewarded; I am there to create an experience for my audience."

Are you willing to create that experience?

# Chapter Eleven

# Speech Topic Ideas

**A** *Speech Topic* is the first and foremost item that needs to be finalized for your presentation. In the past, sometimes, I thought, anything and everything could be a speech topic but most of the time, I felt all the topics were already taken! When I think about it now, I laugh at myself.

Let us understand the below blueprint for finding a perfect speech topic.

Step 1: Larger purpose of the speech

Some questions you can ask to find the larger purpose:

1. Why are you giving the speech?

2. What is the occasion for the speech?

3. What type of speech will suit my larger purpose?

Step 2: Topics that interest YOU

Some questions to find your interest:

1. What do you know?

2. What are you enthusiastic about?

3. What are your life experiences?

Step 3: Topics that interest your AUDIENCE

Some questions to find your audience's interest:

1. What are your audience's needs?

2. Do they belong to a certain age group?

3. What are their shared experiences?

Find what is common in the answers to the questions given under the above three steps. The intersection of the above three steps will be the sweet spot of finding a 'PERFECT TOPIC'.

The general or larger purpose of any speech can be classified into the following four types of speeches.

1. Informational

2. Entertaining

3. Persuasive

4. Inspirational

Based on the above list, do you get an idea of your speech's larger purpose? If not, go back to Step 1 and answer the questions. You should at least be able to tell what type of speech suits your needs. Assuming your general or larger purpose is set, let us explore topic ideas that could overlap your interest and your audience's interest so that you end up with the perfect 'speech topic' idea.

**Informational Speeches:** As the name suggests, these are speeches about a specific subject. You will give an informational speech when your objective is to help the audience gain knowledge on a particular subject, or strengthen their current knowledge level. Example: Project findings, 'How-to' speeches

To present an informational speech, you need to know a subject. But it does not mean that you should have done a post-doctorate in the subject. I am pretty sure you might be an expert in something or the other. The simple question you can ask is, "Are my audience members 'uninformed' about a particular subject?'" Then ask a question, "How will this topic help my audience?" The moment you ask this question, you will start thinking from your audience's perspective and you will know the appropriate information to be used in the speech. Let us explore some ideas for informational speeches.

When will you give a speech? When you are excited, right? But you will only be excited when the topic piques your interest. But the question that stops us from selecting a topic is: What if the audience is not interested in the topic? I agree, not all the things that might interest you will be a suitable speech topic. So, let us explore some ideas, which are largely relatable to everyone.

*Books*: Assuming you are a book reader, can you speak about why one should keep reading books? Can you write 5 major benefits of reading books? Depending on the audience's age group, can you suggest different options? Can you talk about your favorite book? Can you inform about the importance of reading a particular book?

*Gardening*: If Gardening is your area of interest, can you write a speech on why gardening? Can you give tips on how to maintain a good garden? What are all the features of a good garden? What are the benefits of a good garden? Does it give you joy? What are the challenges? Every question in itself can lead to a speech of its own. Think about it.

*Exercise*: Can you talk about the 3 to 5 major benefits of regular exercise? How have you benefited from it? How does it help you in your day-to-day activities? What are the options available for proper exercise in the present-day hectic scenario? What dieting habits to follow when you are in an exercise program? Take these questions in the direction you want. You *will* come up with an idea for your speech.

**Entertaining Speeches:** People like to laugh and if you can make them laugh from the stage, you will go a long way as a speaker. You can convey a point in a straightforward way or in an entertaining way. You might have seen speeches, which are given entertainingly. Stand-up acts will fall under the entertaining speech category. Humorous speeches also fall under the entertaining speech category. These are speeches where you want the audience to have a good time. Let us face it. If you want the audience to have a good time, you have to make them laugh. Stand-up acts, humorous speeches, feel good inspiring speeches will fall under this category. Let us explore some ideas for entertaining speeches.

*Largely Relatable Unexpected Events:*

Let us understand this with an example. Let us say, you are a guy and you are going on a date. Or, maybe you are a girl and you are taking a guy on a date. (Let us not rule this out!) On the way, your vehicle ran out of fuel. And it turned out to be the worst date. I am pretty sure; you will share this incident with your buddies at the coffee table. Just note the way you describe the incidents to your friends. Note down the instances and sentences at which they laugh. Jot down the exact sentences. It will be easier to create an entertaining speech.

*Unusual Physical Traits:*

Your physical traits are what the audience will see in the first place. If someone else uses your physical trait, then it becomes offensive. If you self-depreciate your physical trait, it is comedy! Just think about what is unique about your appearance. Are you very tall, good-looking, not so good-looking? Write down instances where you had embarrassing experiences / funny experiences because of that trait. Let us see an example. I have seen a speech, where the speaker won the Humorous Speech Championship at Toastmasters just with one idea. 'He was short'. He constructed the whole plot with his height. He shared his embarrassment since he was a child. He cited funny incidents at school and in public places. He described his relationship with his wife who was taller than him. It was a laughter riot. What ideas does this give you?

Are you dark in color? I don't want you to spark any racist feelings. Only if others talk about your color, it can be called as racism. If 'you' joke about your color, it is not racism. There must be certain instances where you were embarrassed or had unique experiences because of your color. This could be your idea for an entertaining speech topic.

*Your Current Life Situation:*

Think about your current life situation. Whatever stage of life you are currently in, you can easily form topics. For example, are you a teenager? You can talk about your experience with your 'girl' friends. It does not mean, you need to have one. Even if you don't have one, write how hard it is to get one. If you have a girlfriend, write how hard it is to maintain one!

Are you in your 20s? Can you talk about your quarter-life crisis? Maybe you are not happy with your job. Maybe you don't want to get married. Maybe you want to get married but are scared. Maybe you're married. Do you think your everyday life has material for an entertaining speech? Just complain!

Even if you are in your 30s, 40s, or 50s, I am sure some part of your current life situation worries you. Write about it. By being real and authentic, you build trust and credibility with the audience. This is very important to create humor. And humor is the main ingredient in an entertaining speech.

**Persuasive Speeches:** These are speeches to persuade the audience to accept your point of view. These speeches make the audience think, act, or feel your point. These speeches are powerful, as you will have to deal with the psychology of the audience. If you have seen Barack Obama's acceptance or nomination speeches, they are perfect examples of persuasive speeches. Humor is also usually used in a persuasive speech. Motivational humorists use humor to entertain and persuade the audience at the same time. For persuasive speeches, you need to convince the audience to take some action or change their perception based on your point. I think most of the people today need someone else to confirm what is the right thing to do. And when you tap into this fact, you will easily find speech topics for persuasion. Before we explore topic ideas for persuasive speeches, it is a good idea to know about ethos, pathos, and logos. The great philosopher Aristotle coined these terms. These are the different elements involved in persuasion. In a nutshell:

1. *Ethos* relates to the credibility quotient: being fair, using proper language, using correct grammar, and using appropriate vocabulary.

2. *Pathos* relates to the emotional quotient: emotional tone, stories of emotional events

3. *Logos* relates to the logical quotient: facts or figures, citing history, and logical arguments.

Ideally, every persuasive/inspiring speech should have these three elements in the right proportions. I believe that ethos and pathos play a very important role in a persuasive/inspiring speech. By far the best way to incorporate ethos and pathos is to tell a personal Story. Mark Brown, 1995 World Champion of Public Speaking said, 'Your life tells a story and there is someone out there who needs to hear it'.

*What are your core values?* List them down. *Who taught them to you? When did that happen? What are the things you used to believe in?* List them down. Did any particular incident change those beliefs? When did that happen? How did that 'change', change your life? What were the most painful periods in your life? How did you overcome them? What did you learn from them? *What is your message?*

**Inspirational Speeches:** These are speeches that will help your audience reach their highest potential. You need to change the way the audience' thinks/feels or acts after listening to your speech. You aim to convince the audience to do noble things or follow greater ideologies. You have already explored topics in the earlier sections, but instead of persuading your audience to agree with your viewpoint; your core focus is to inspire them to new possibilities. Once, my mentor *Jerry Aiyathurai* gave me a tip. He asked me, *to write down three surprises of my life*. When I did, I got an idea that led to another, and *Bing*, I got an idea for an inspiring speech.

What about you? *Can you write down the three surprises of your life?* What did you learn from it?

Hope this chapter was useful for you.

**<u>Just a surprise for you:</u>**

Grab the free download of the entire *Public Speaking Topic Secrets* audiobook to find your perfect speech topic idea at http://publicspeakking.com/toastmasterssecret/

# Chapter Twelve

# To Do Before, During and After the Speech

I n this chapter, we'll discuss specific steps one can take whether you are living a regular day with no deadline for speech delivery, or you have a deadline (D-day) for speech delivery.

**What to do on a regular day (when you do not have a speech D-day):**

1. Collecting ideas: When you are chatting with a friend or a relative, you might get an idea or an interesting observation. Write it down in a notebook (call it "Ideas Notebook").

2. Work on Your Regular Voice: While practicing and speaking one-on-one with people, start speaking from your diaphragm (your stomach area).

3. Breathing exercises: Do simple and regular breathing exercises.

4. Stance correction: When you stand and speak with anyone, maintain: a straight spine, broad shoulders, open chest, and equal weight on both feet

**What to do when you have a few weeks before the D-day:**

1 Find your speech rate (*number of words spoken per minute*). For example, if I had a script of 500 words and I took 5 minutes to complete that speech, then my speech rate is 100 words/minute. Speaking rate and allotted time will determine the right number of words for your script. Hence, if I want to give an 8-minute speech, I will need 800 words (multiply 8 by 100) in my speech. This is my desired word count.

2. Refer to your Ideas Notebook or refer to the Speech Topic Ideas section to start with a speech.

3. Write your speech draft and work till you meet all the objectives of the speech project.

4. Check for the word count of the speech. Maybe your word count is 1,200 words but your desired value is 800. You can get the word count to the desired level by chipping away unwanted words or parts. Read every sentence of your speech. Check if the main message is still clear without that sentence. If it is, then strike it off. Speech writing is like sculpting a statue. How do we do that? Cut down stories, which are not add any value or new dimension to your main message. Use dialogues instead of narration.

5. Once you are good with the script, imagine the actual presentation room where you'd be delivering your speech on D-day.

6. When you are back at your usual practice location, close your eyes and imagine the D-day presentation room is filled with an audience. With your eyes still closed, start practicing

your speech using the below steps.

a. Stand with a straight back; keep your hands to the side with your fingers slightly curled; keep your feet at around 12 inches distance from each other. At this point, you need not worry about eye contact, gesturing, movement, facial expressions, or voice modulation. *Practice till your speech script is in your muscle memory.* Then follow the below steps in sequence:

b. Practice eye contact by looking at the imaginary audience.

c. Practice physical movements in your speech. Work on your staging: determine your footwork; place your characters on stage and practice till you get it right.

d. Let your hands gesture naturally. Use more of open palm gestures, raise your hand from shoulder level, and avoid pointed gestures.

e. Ask your friend or Toastmaster to give feedback on expressions and practice till you get them right. Check whether your facial expressions match the intent of each sentence of your speech.

f. Check if you complete every word before you go to the next word. Make sure you end the words properly.

g. Find your optimum tone by practicing in a tone ranging from soft to loud, and fast to slow.

h. Add emotions to your speech. If your content should make your audience feel happy, you should also feel happiness. If your content should make the audience feel sad, you should also feel sadness.

7. Finally practice by incorporating all the above points. I bet you will be awesome. Record this practice on the computer

and try to find any distracting mechanisms. Give a complete rehearsal to your close friends, family, or anyone who would listen to your speech.

**What to do during the D-day:**

1. Eat simple food. Breads and salads will work fine. You need energy to show energy in your speech!

2. Ask your club member or fellow Toastmaster to record your speech.

3. Do a quick visualization practice: Close your eyes and imagine the presentation room filled with the audience. Rehearse and check if the speech flows.

4. Get excited to deliver your speech.

5. A minute before you are called on stage, your heart might race, your hands might shiver, your legs might wobble, you might feel the urge to go to the restroom, and all weird things will happen.

a. Here's how you tackle them at a physical level: Rub your left palm with your right hand for 10-15 seconds and vice versa. Bring your heart rate to normal. Slowly, breathe in and breathe out.

b. How to tackle them at a mental level? Answer the following questions (learned from Darren LaCroix, 2001 World Champion of Public Speaking): What is my intent? Am I present? Will I have fun? How would I give this presentation if I knew this was the last one ever?

After tackling the last-minute jitters at a physical and mental level, go ahead and enjoy the delivery!

**What to do after the D-day:**

1. After your speech, listen to your evaluations. Get feedback from everyone but only process those, which make sense to you. A caveat, if the feedback comes from a professional or someone who has some level of success in speaking, then you might need to process those even if it does not make sense to you (yet).

2. Call your friend or Toastmaster and get the video recording. Do you exhibit any of the following behaviors?

· Hand shivers

· Wobbling of legs

· Repetitive gesturing of hands

· Walking left and right like a pendulum

· Shifting weight of body on right or left leg at regular intervals

· Slouchy shoulders

· Looking down during the speech

· Not making eye contact with the audience or looking at the ceiling

· Monotone voice

· Having tense facial expressions while narrating a pleasant experience

· Laughing even before the audience laughs after telling a joke

· Not showing emotions that correspond to the intent of the message

3. Identify the areas of distraction in your delivery and start working to remove them in your next speech preparation.

# Conclusion

Congratulations on completing the book! It takes commitment to finish what you start.

Speaking and communication is a continuous process. Start speaking at every opportunity. It could be at your club, workplace, or social gatherings. Look around, and you will find opportunities. Apply your learnings when you are speaking. Your confidence and self-esteem will increase multifold when these learnings are put to use.

Let me know your comments, suggestions, and progress by leaving a review on Amazon or sending a note to Rama@pu blicspeakKing.com.

Keep Smiling, Keep Rocking, and Happy Public Speaking!

**Ramakrishna Reddy**

# Q&A with Author

**1. What's the one thing I can do to take advantage of my tenure in Toastmasters?**

Put the work to complete the speech projects. Apart from that, if you ask me for one thing, I'd suggest that you compete in speech contests. It's a humbling experience and will help assess your real progress. If you compete and lose in a contest, you still win. You lose when you don't compete at all.

**2. What made you write this book?**

I've mentored hundreds of Toastmasters, and one common thing I noticed is that they needed a reference to a real speech to show how different objectives/techniques have been implemented. That's what made me write this book. And I'm happy that it worked out well because several thousand people have benefitted from this book so far.

**3. Why do you care about public speaking?**

I truly believe that this skill can change your life for good. Why? It gives you something that can't be bought ready-made. And that something is **confidence**. I'm not even talking about confidence on the stage and having the power to talk to hundreds or thousands of people. I'm talking about the power to do other things that you may find meaningful. I wrote this book because of the confidence I gained through public speaking. If I can help people learn this skill as a starting point, I believe it'll transform their lives. And this is exciting for me.

### 4. Hey, I love this book. How can I support you as a reader?

Thank you for picking up this book. This means a lot to me. If you want to support me, please share this work with your friends, social media, or anyone who needs public speaking help. Also, you can write an honest Amazon review (you can use the below link to share your review). Thank you for being awesome!

https://www.amazon.com/review/create-review?&asin=B00TOOOJRQ

### 5. Do you have a course related to public speaking?

Yes, public speaking is better learned when you see them (especially the voice and body language delivery techniques). Precisely, it's for this reason I created a video course to show these key concepts. Please check out the video course in the below link (If it helps at all, please use discount code 50OFF for a 50% discount on the course fee).

https://publicspeakking.gumroad.com/l/37stepsvideocourse

**6. How can I contact you for any further questions or support?**

I'd be happy to help in any way I can. Please reach out to me at Rama@PublicspeakKing.com

Wish You Success,
Ramakrishna Reddy

# Acknowledgements

I would like to thank all the Toastmasters who have helped me in some way or other. My fellow Toastmasters at Infosys Pune Toastmasters Club (Pune, India), Toastmasters at Aetna Speaks Up (Hartford, USA), and my fellow advanced Toastmasters at Central Connecticut Advanced Toastmasters (Berlin, USA).

I kept doing things as if I knew a lot of things about public speaking until I met Jerry Aiyathurai, a TEDx speaker and Toastmasters World Championship finalist. Jerry, you have been more than kind to me. Your message to give forward is still lingering in my head.

I would also like to thank the Champions: Darren LaCroix, 2001 World Champion of Public Speaking; Lance Miller, 2005 World Champion; Dilip Abayasekara, 1992 World Champion Runner-up. I have learned a ton of skills just by watching them and interacting with them.

I want to thank my dad Narayana Reddy for giving me the freedom and wisdom to choose my path in life and excel at it. I would like to pay tribute to my greatest gift, my mom Ammayeammal, who instilled the confidence that I can do better things in life. I would not be who I am if it had not been for my three lovely sisters Leelavathy, Lakshmi, and Indumathy who took care of me after my mom went to heaven.

I would like to thank my dear friends at school and college; you guys rock!

I want to thank Dan Rex, and Sally Newell-Cohen (CxOs from Toastmasters International) for their valuable time in looking into my request for any objection to publishing this book. Your kindness in not objecting to this publication has helped a lot of Toastmasters get access to this book. Thank you once again.

I want to thank Lance Miller, a true world champion and kind-hearted human being, for taking the time to look into this book, and even provide a blurb for me, a first-time author. You are awesome.

I want to thank Charisma Srivastava and Akansha Agarwal, your patience in reviewing and editing the book again and again is commendable.

I want to thank Anu Moudgil and Shikhar Angra. Thank you for the meticulous review and feedback.

I want to thank my cover designer, Samson Mathew. Your umpteen designs made it difficult for me to choose the final one.

I want to thank my technical designer and go-to person, Arun Prabhu. If you had not been there, this work would not have been converted into a book.

Finally, to you, the Reader. You were the actual reason for the creation of this book. If not for you, this whole work would not hold any value.

Keep Smiling, Keep Rocking, and Happy Public Speaking!

Made in the USA
Coppell, TX
09 November 2024

39931391R00065